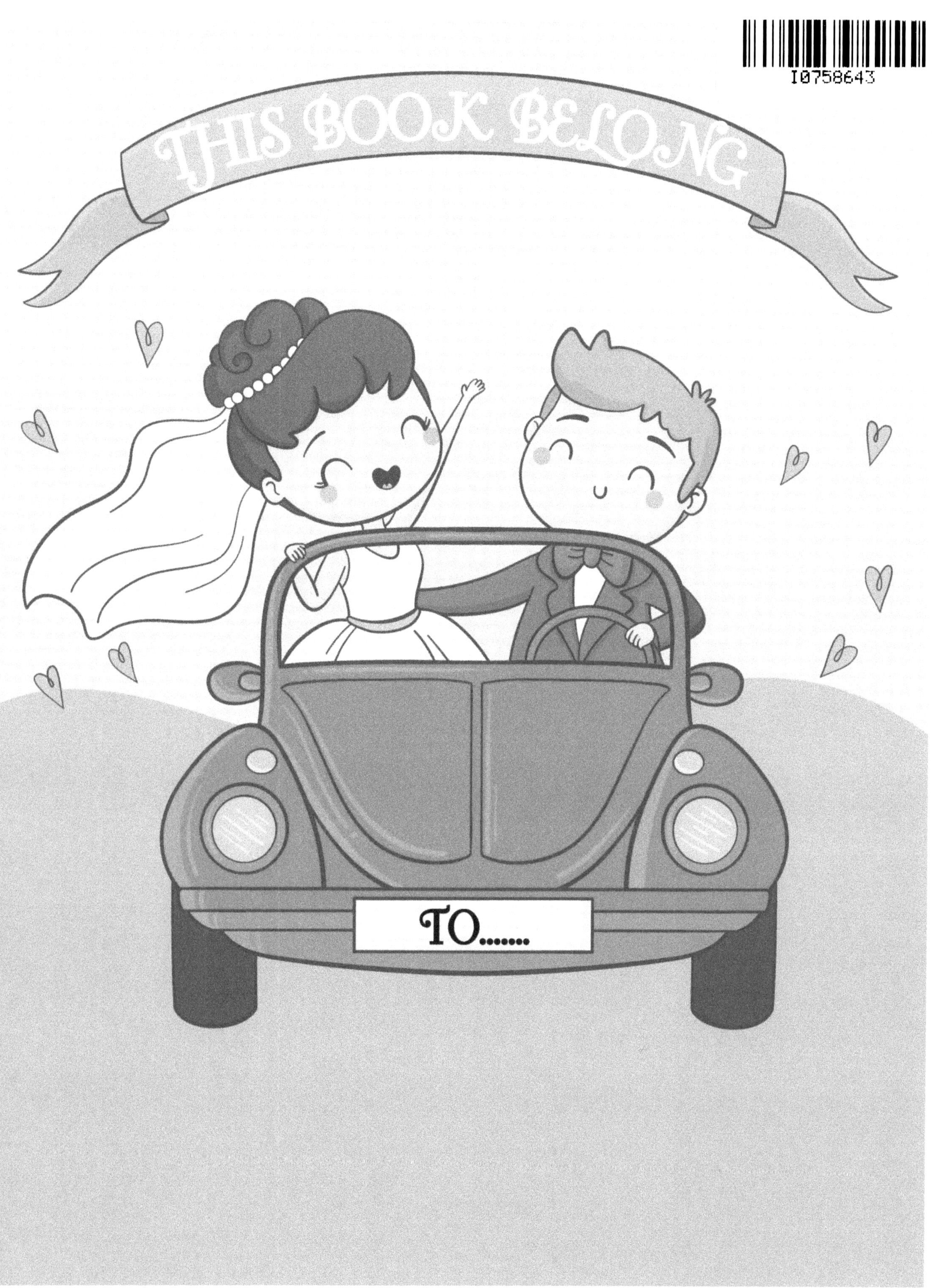

I0758643
THIS BOOK BELONG
TO.......

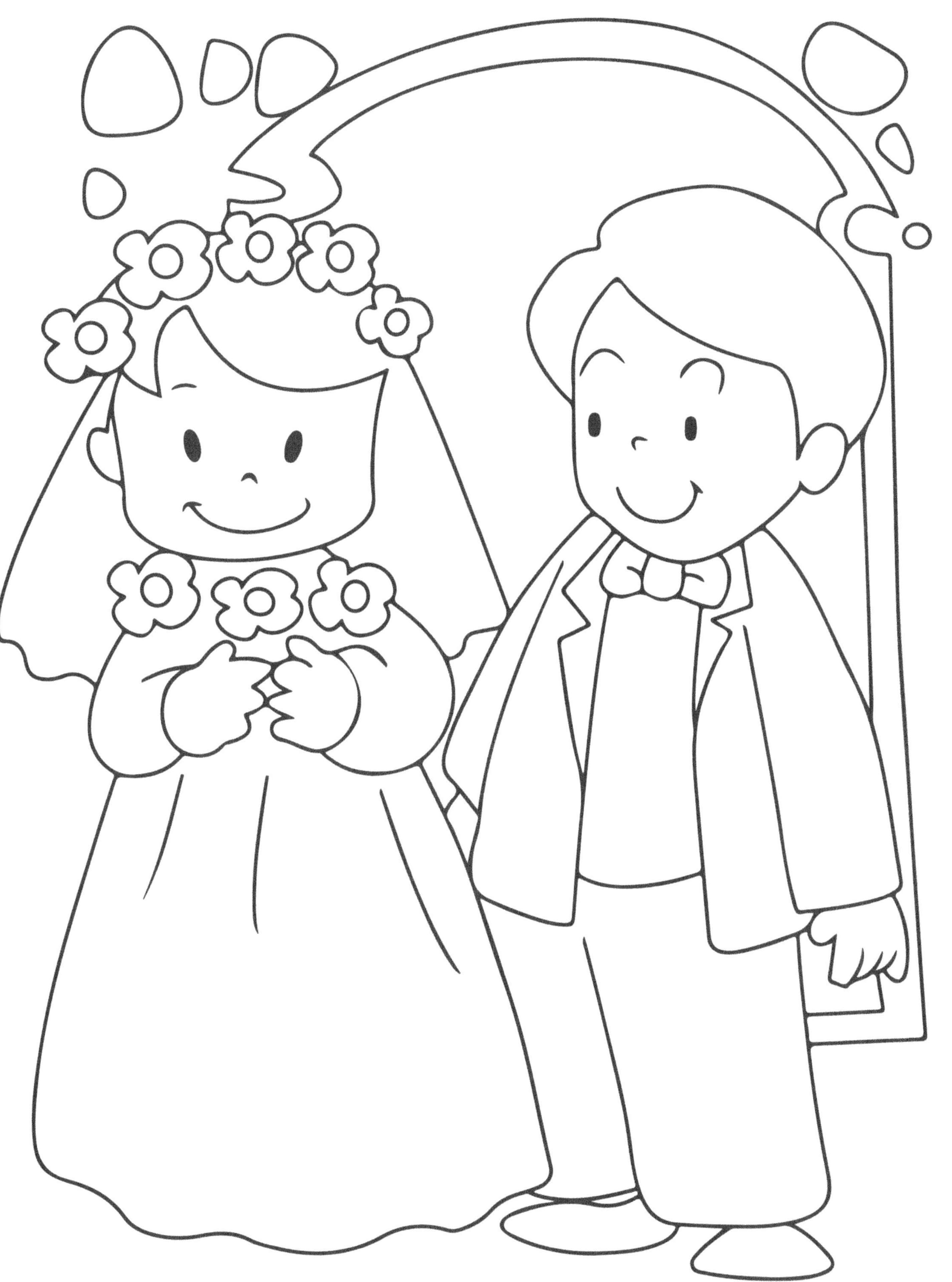

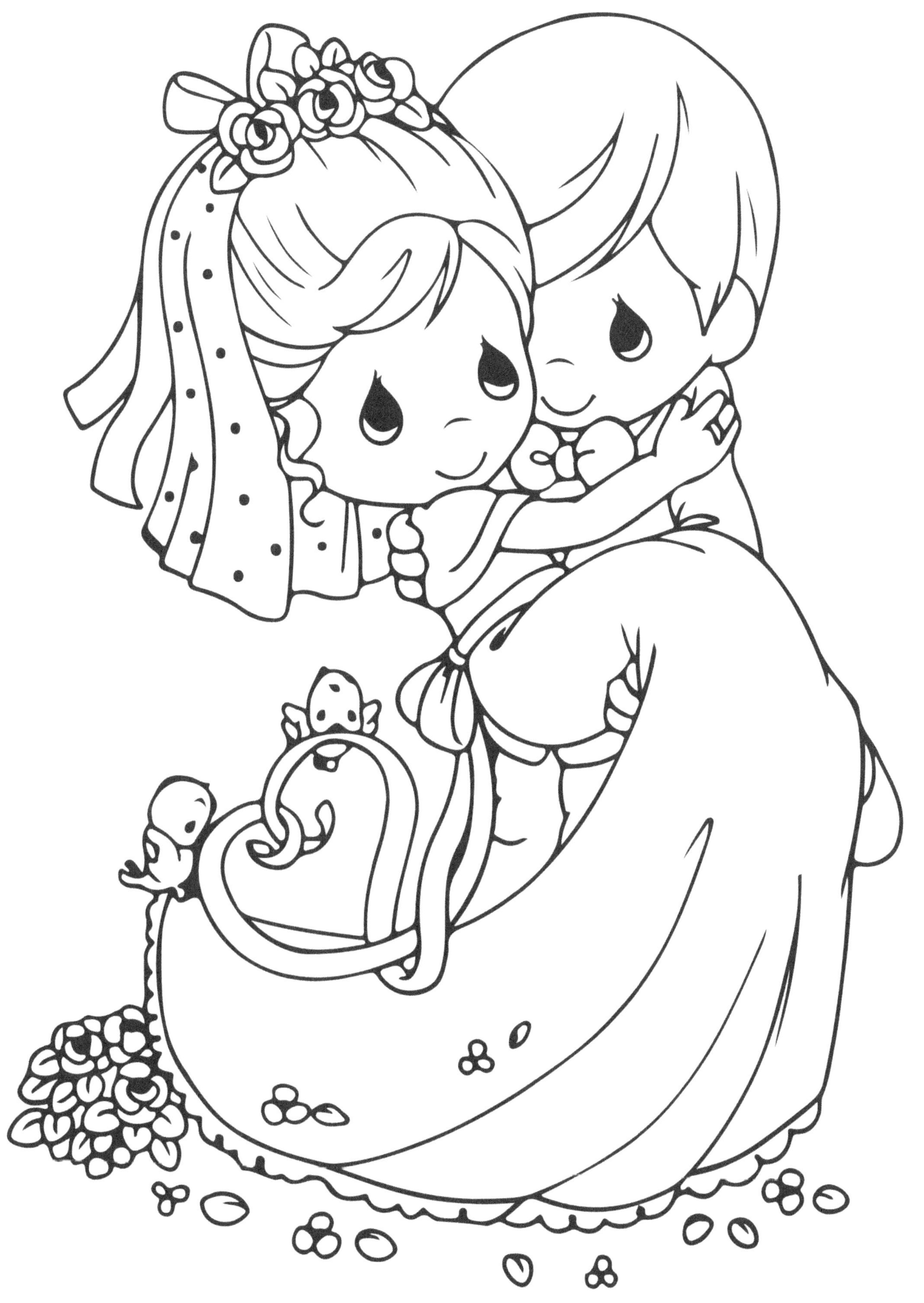

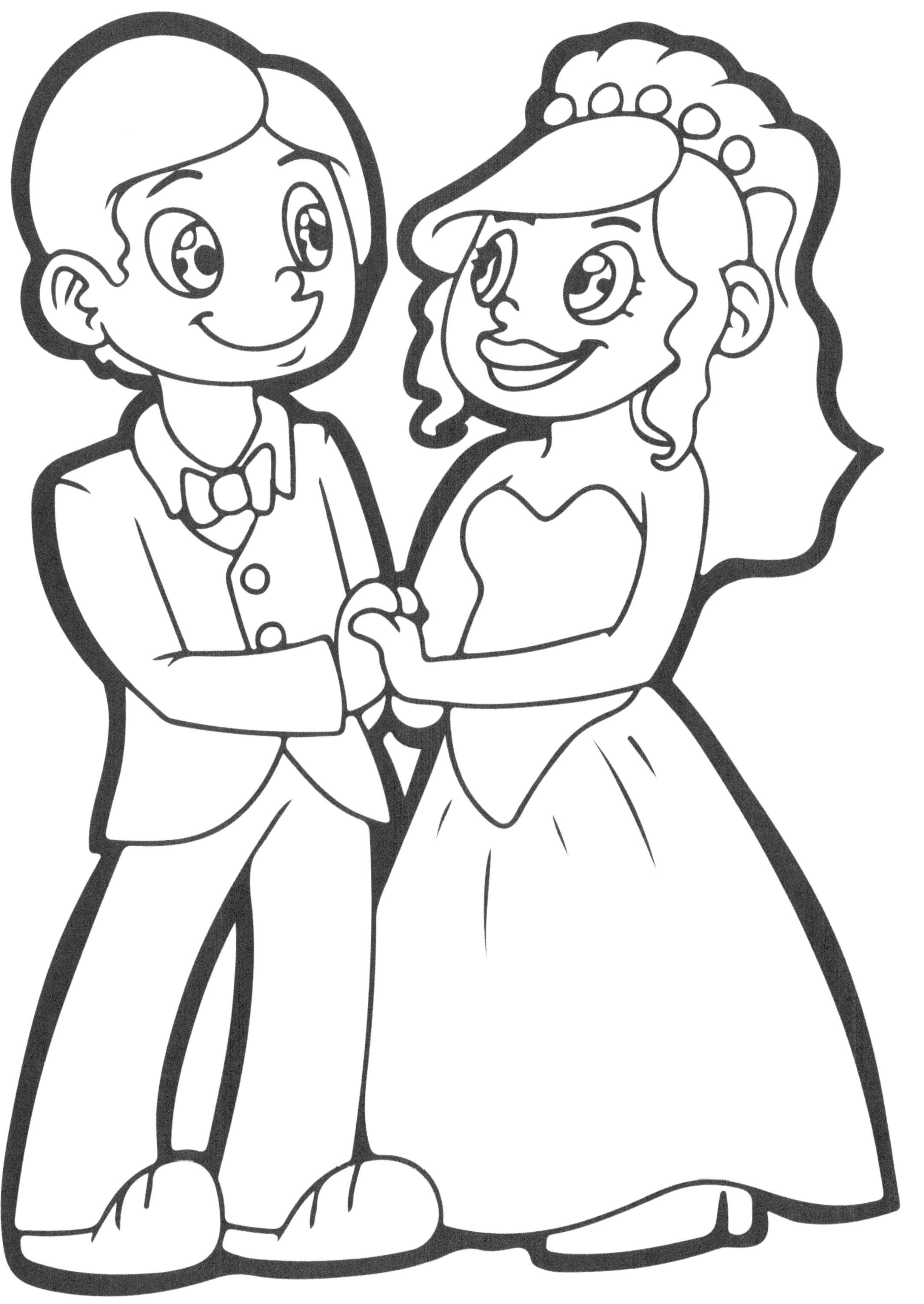

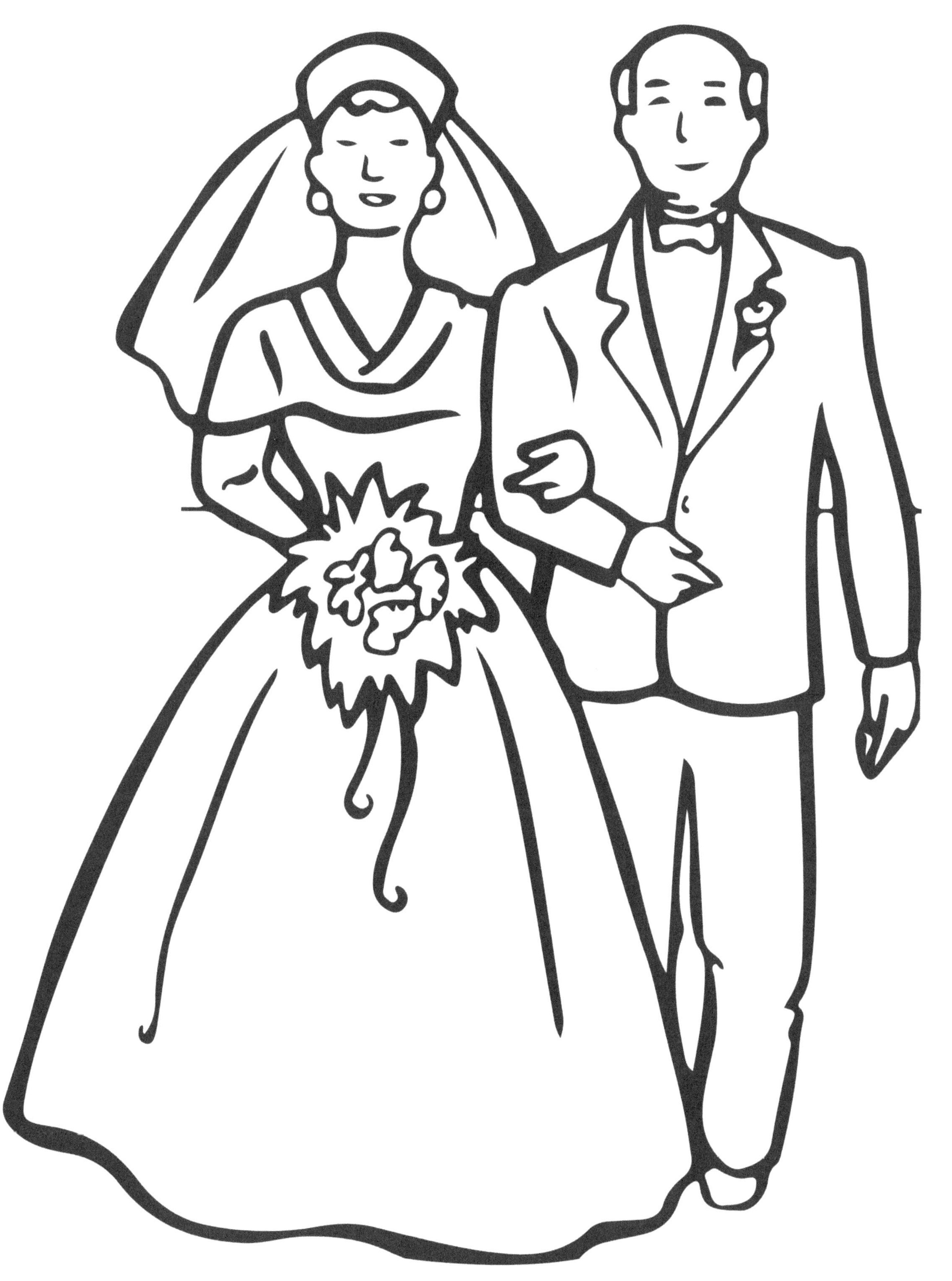

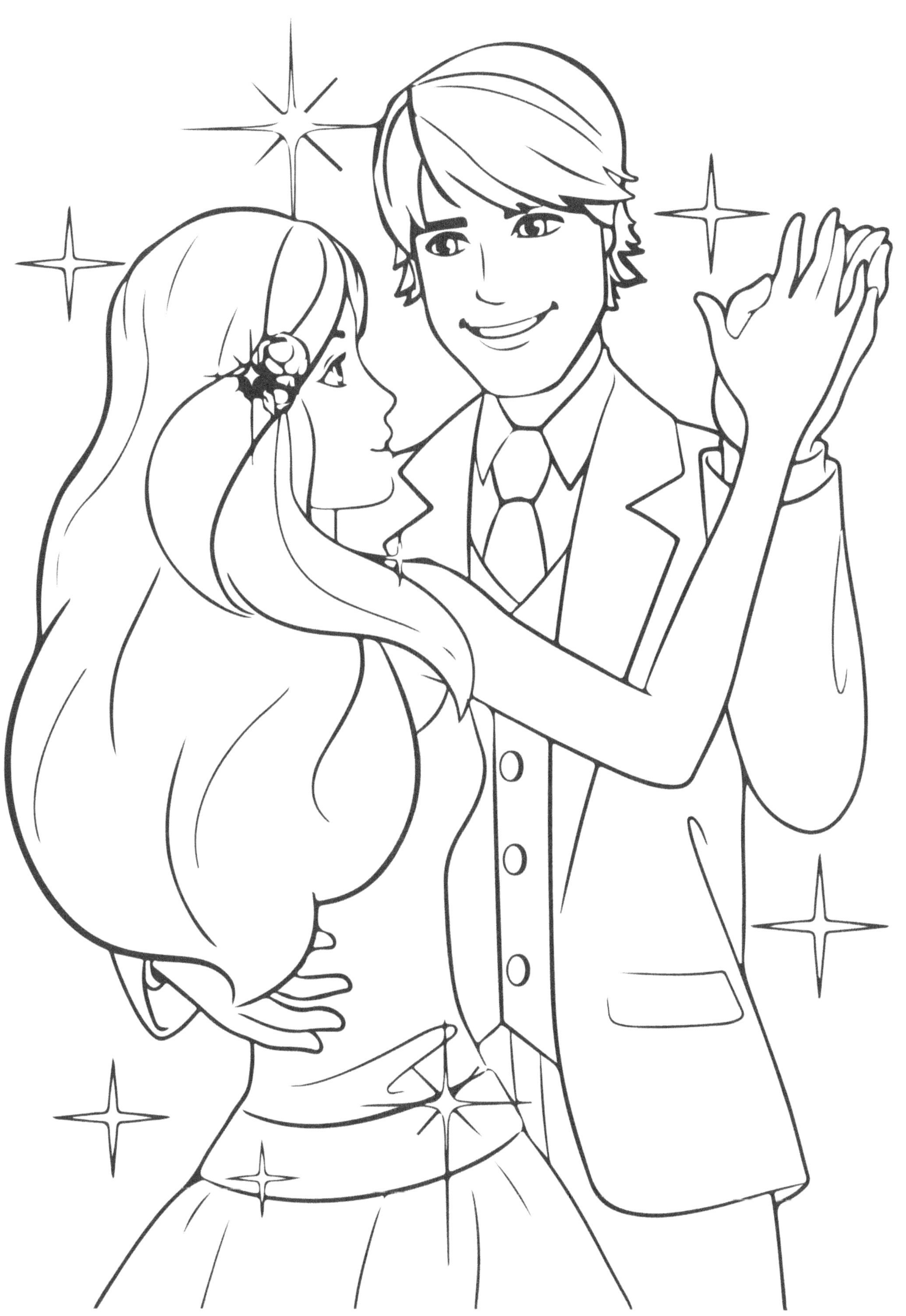

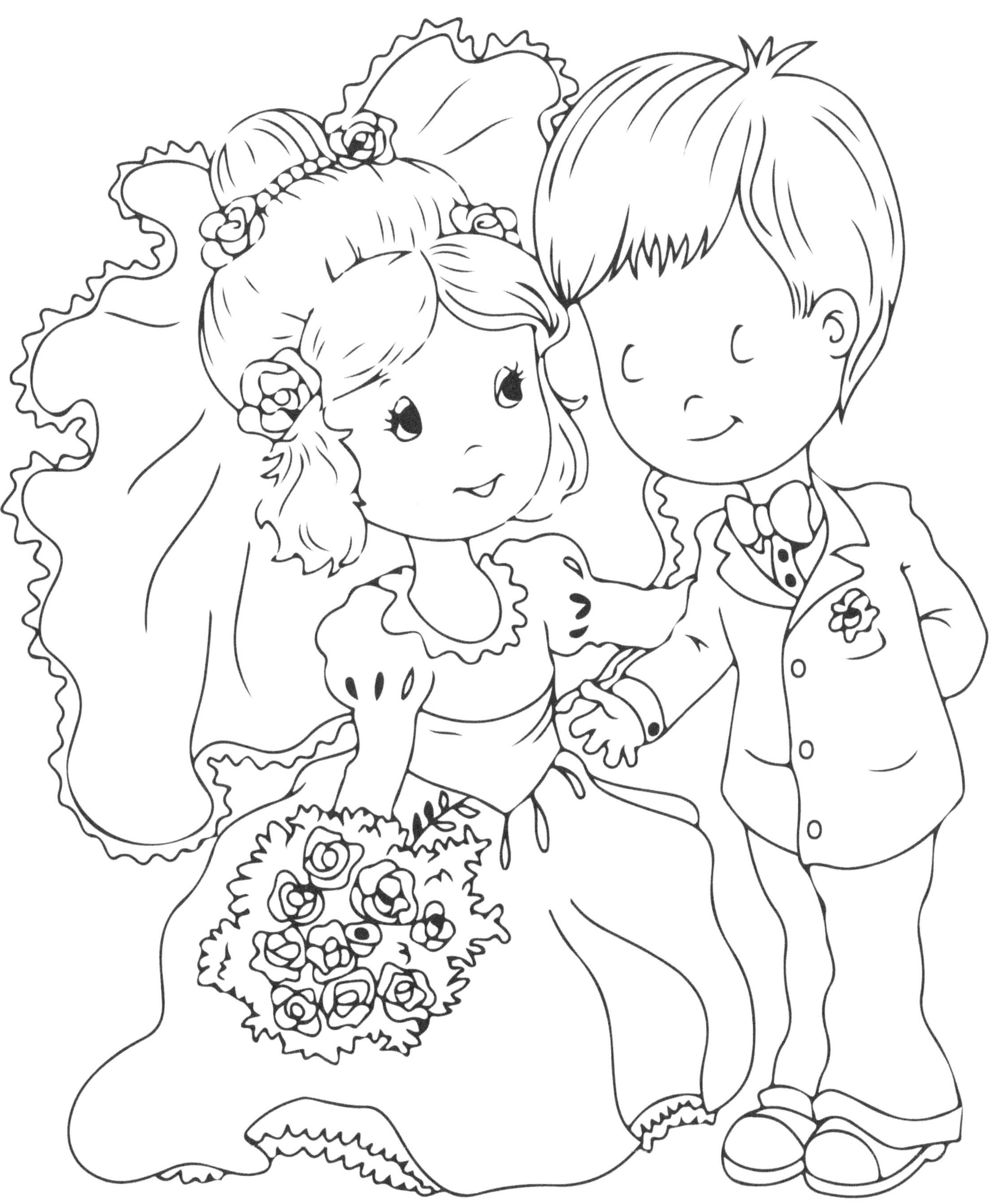

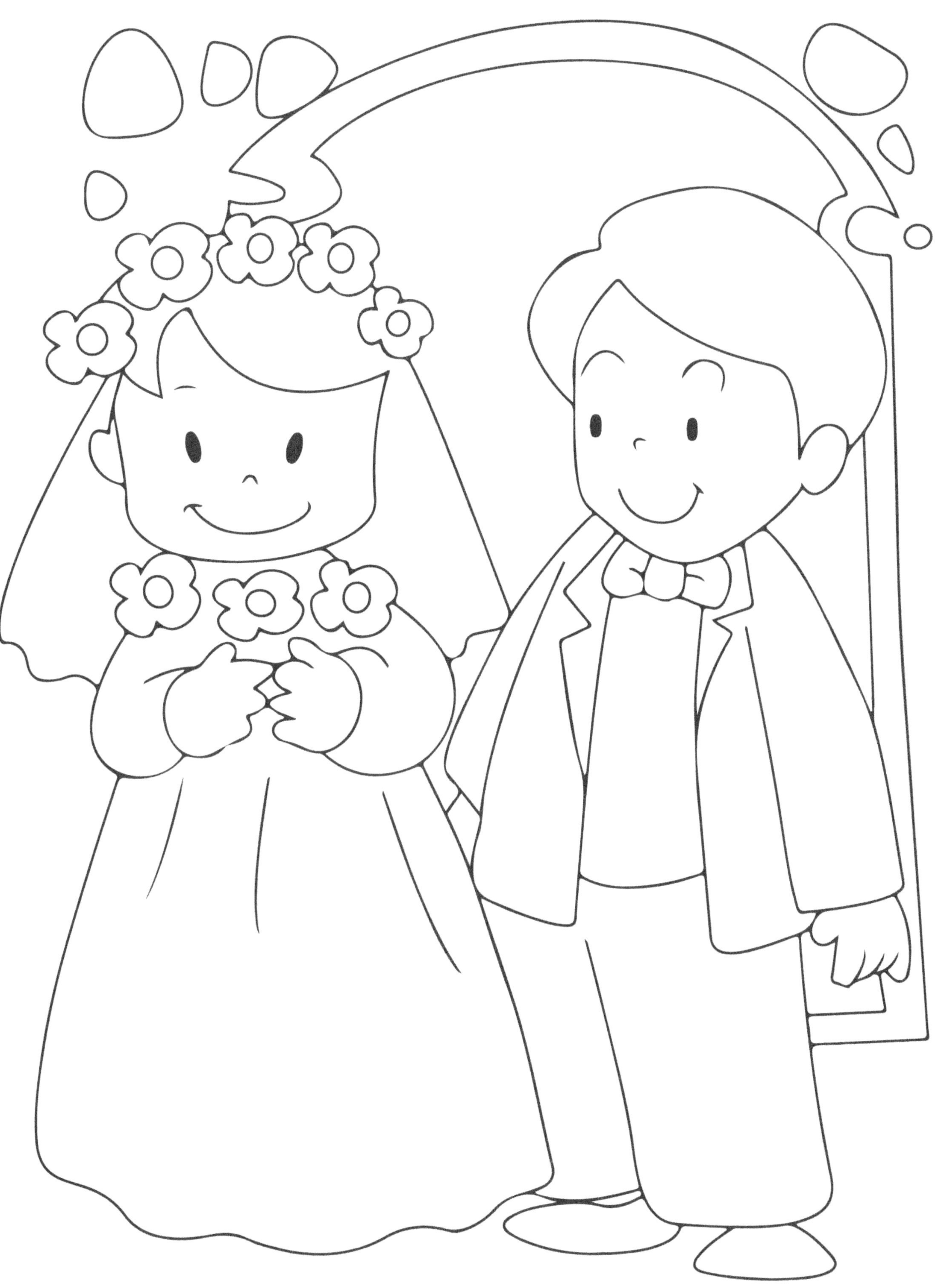

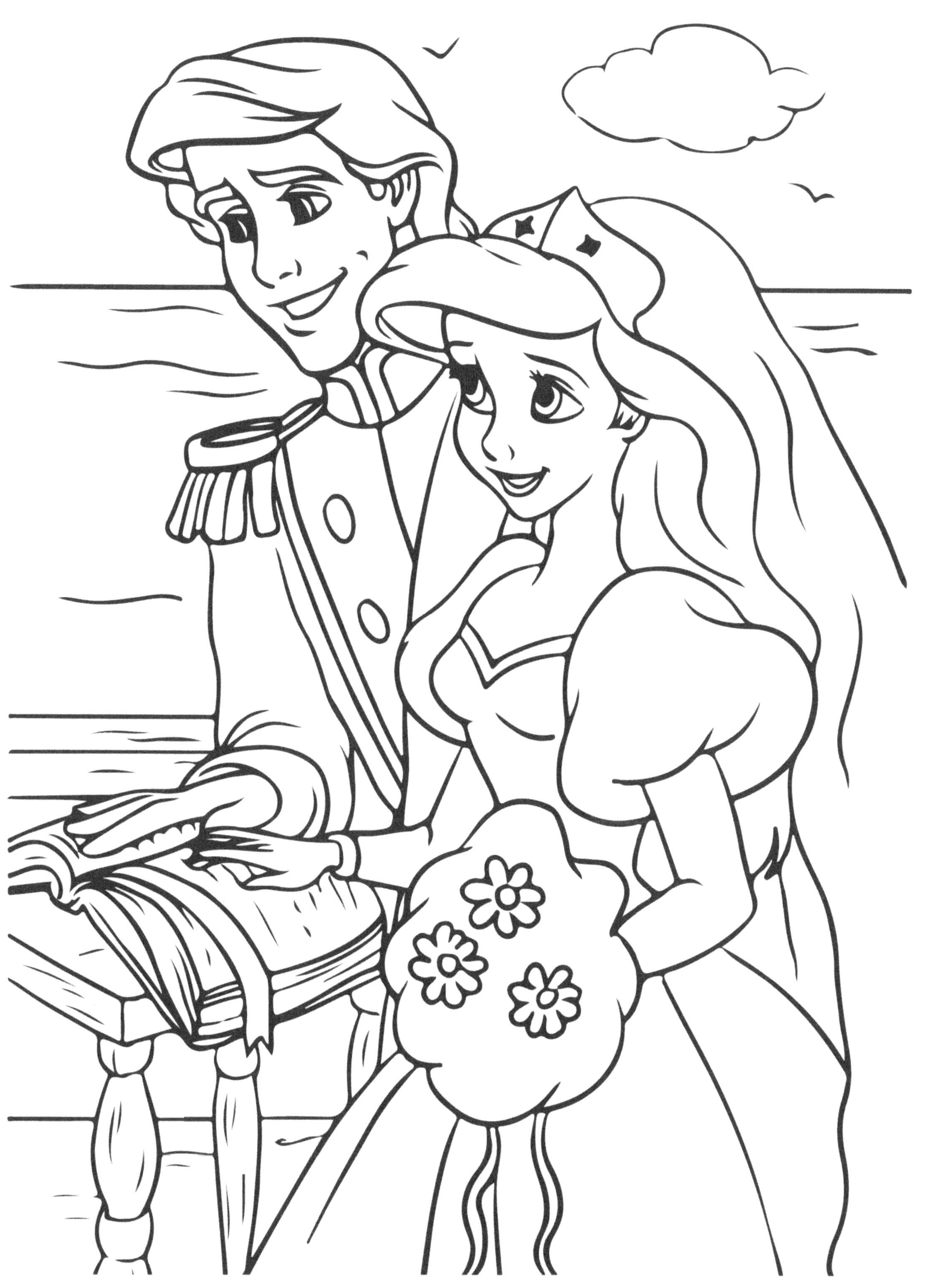

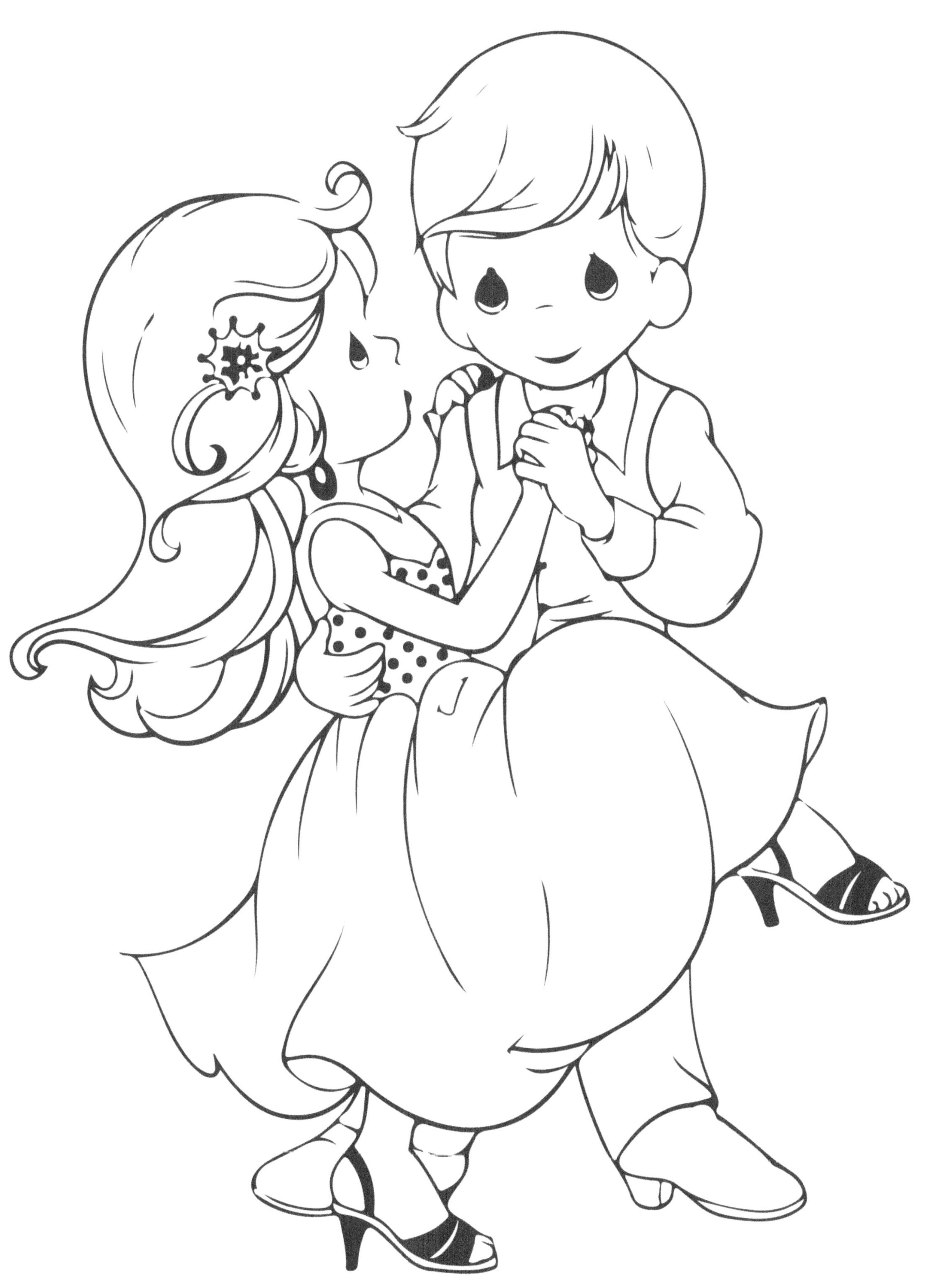

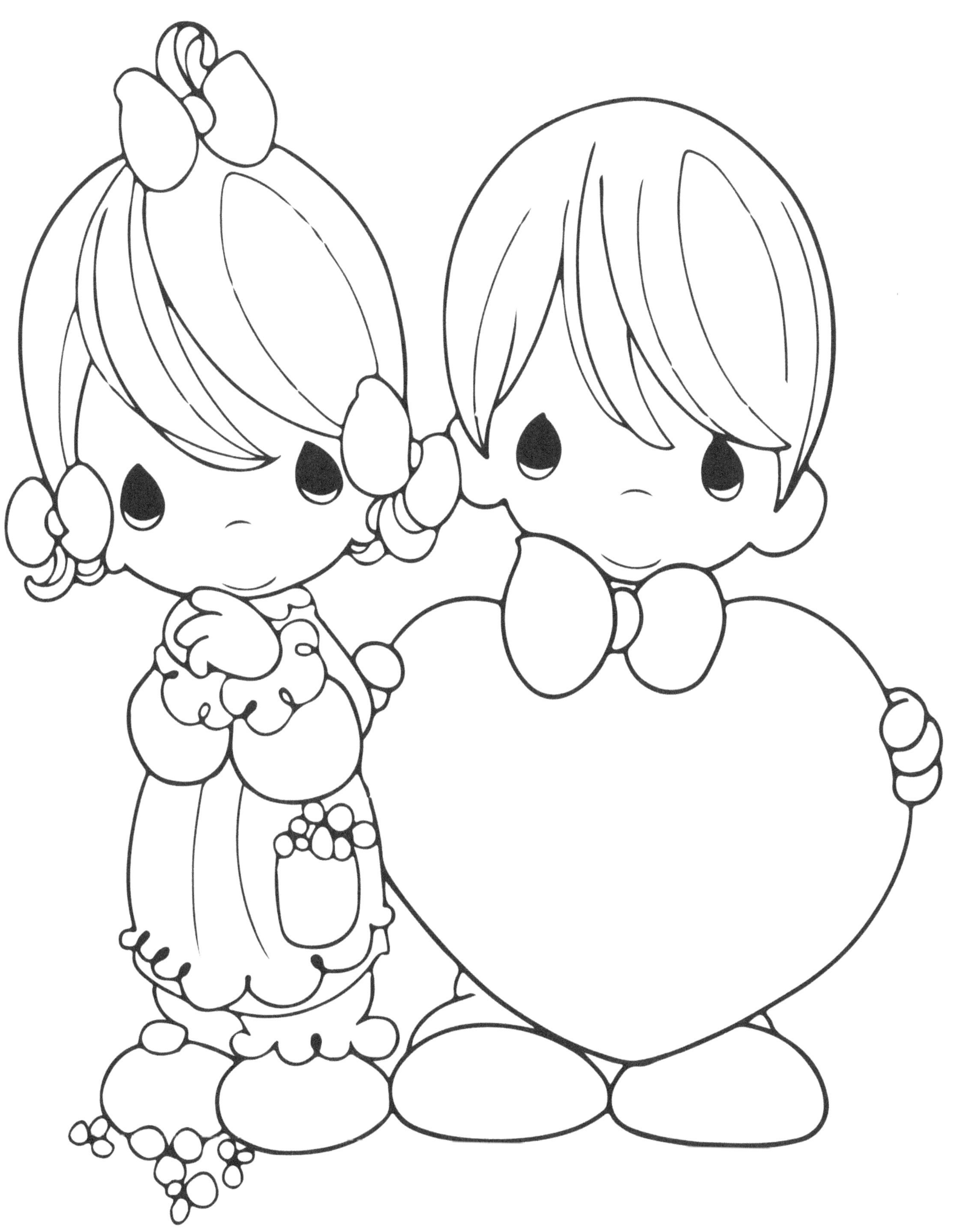

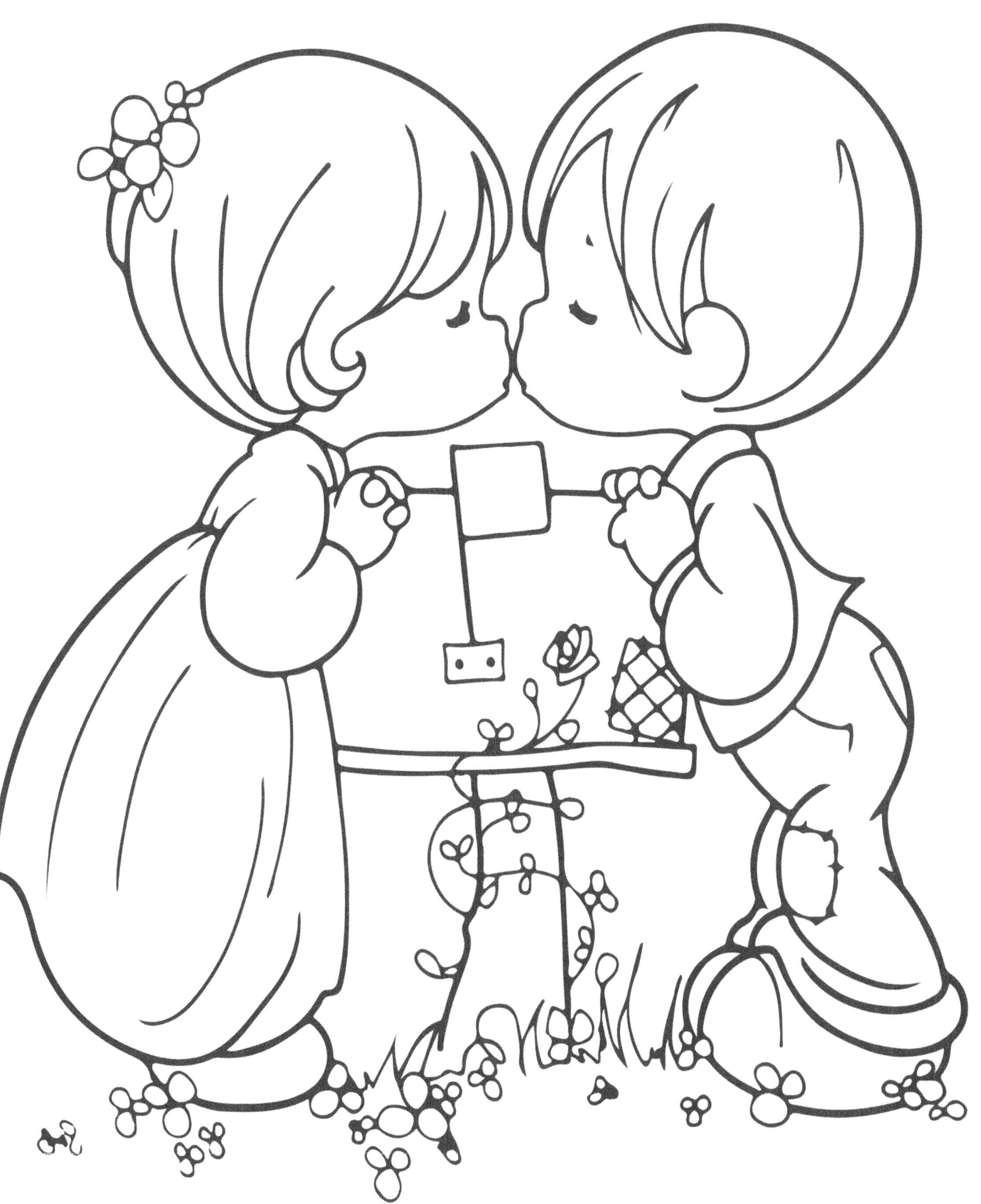

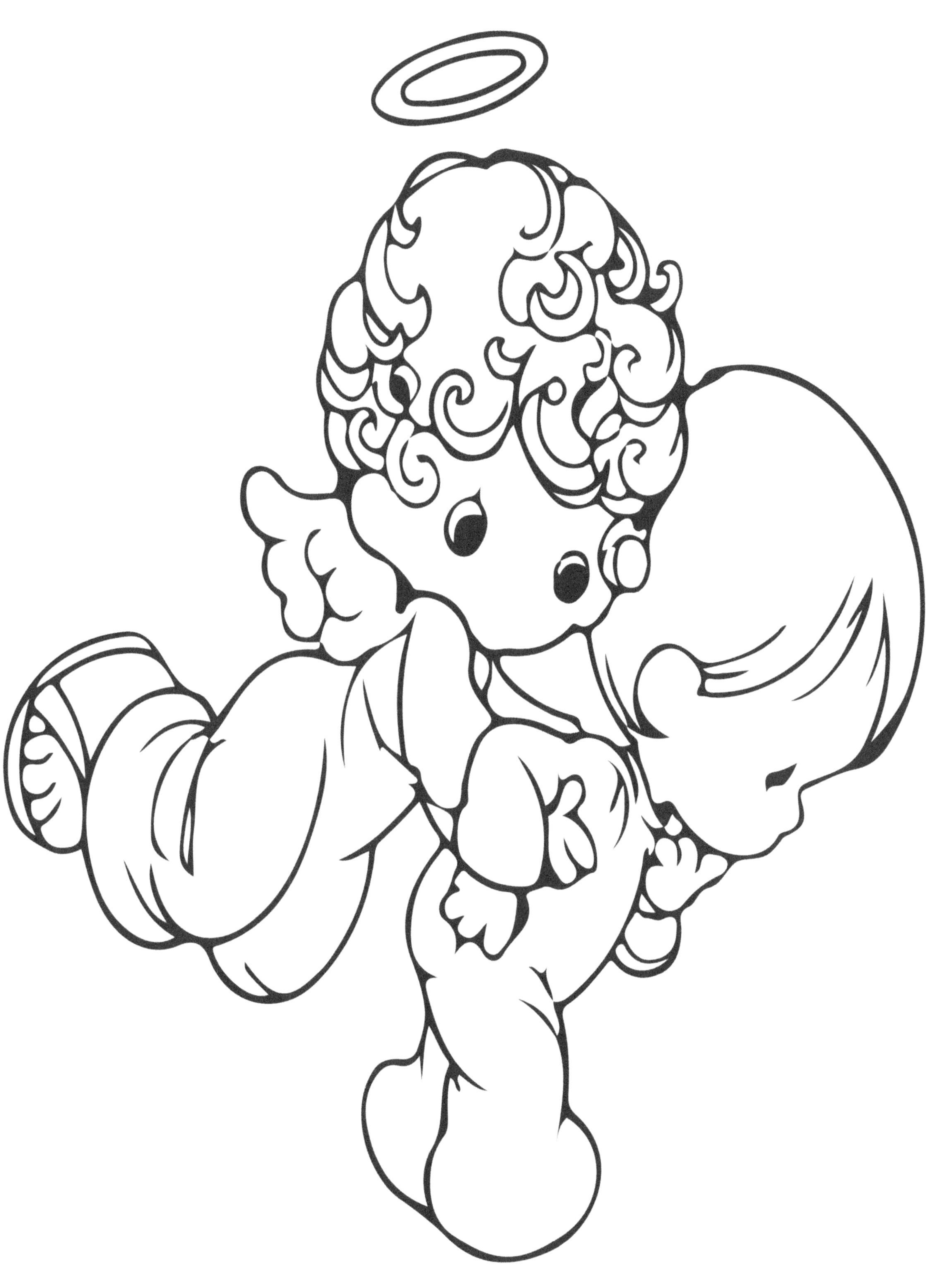

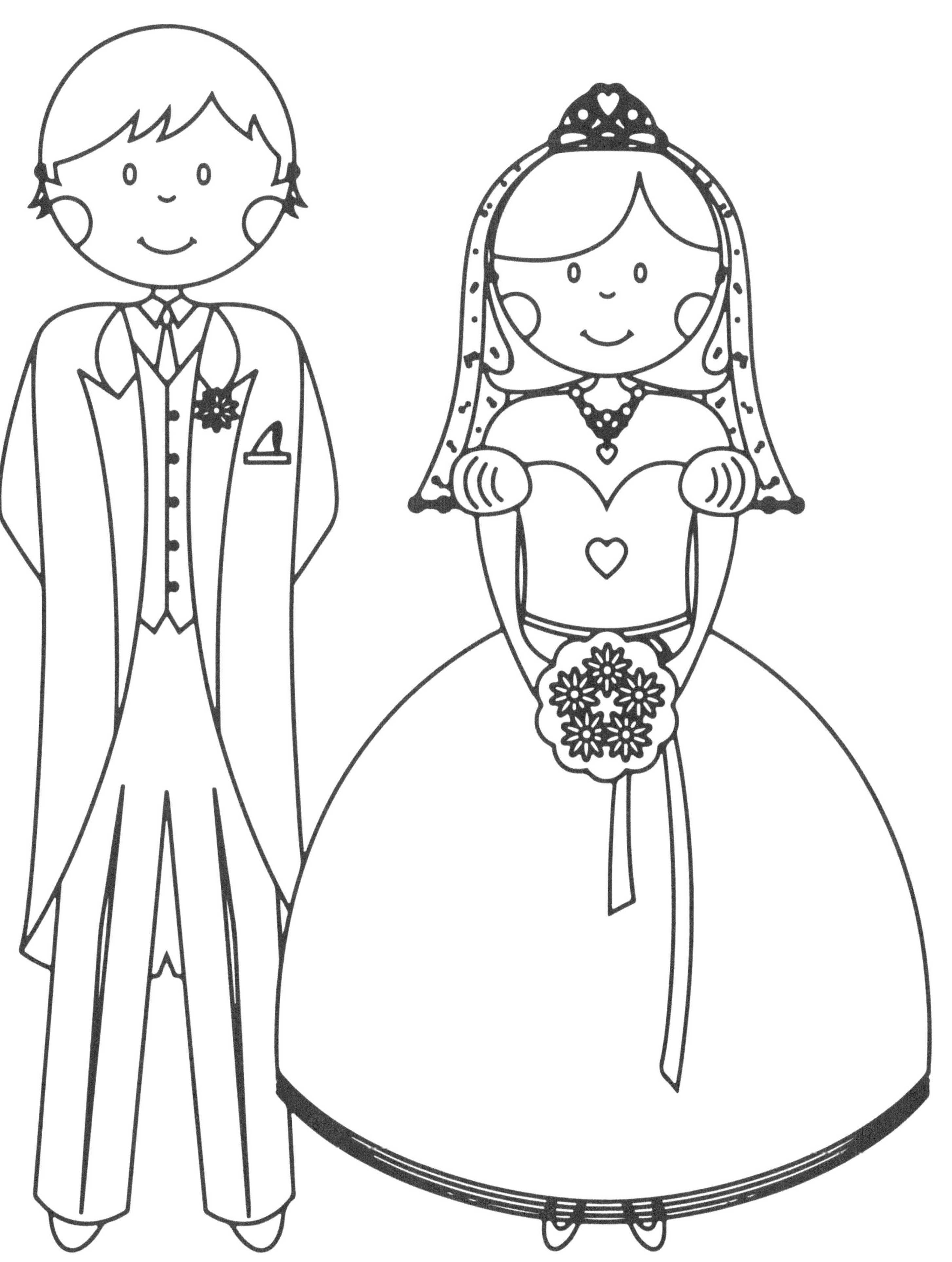

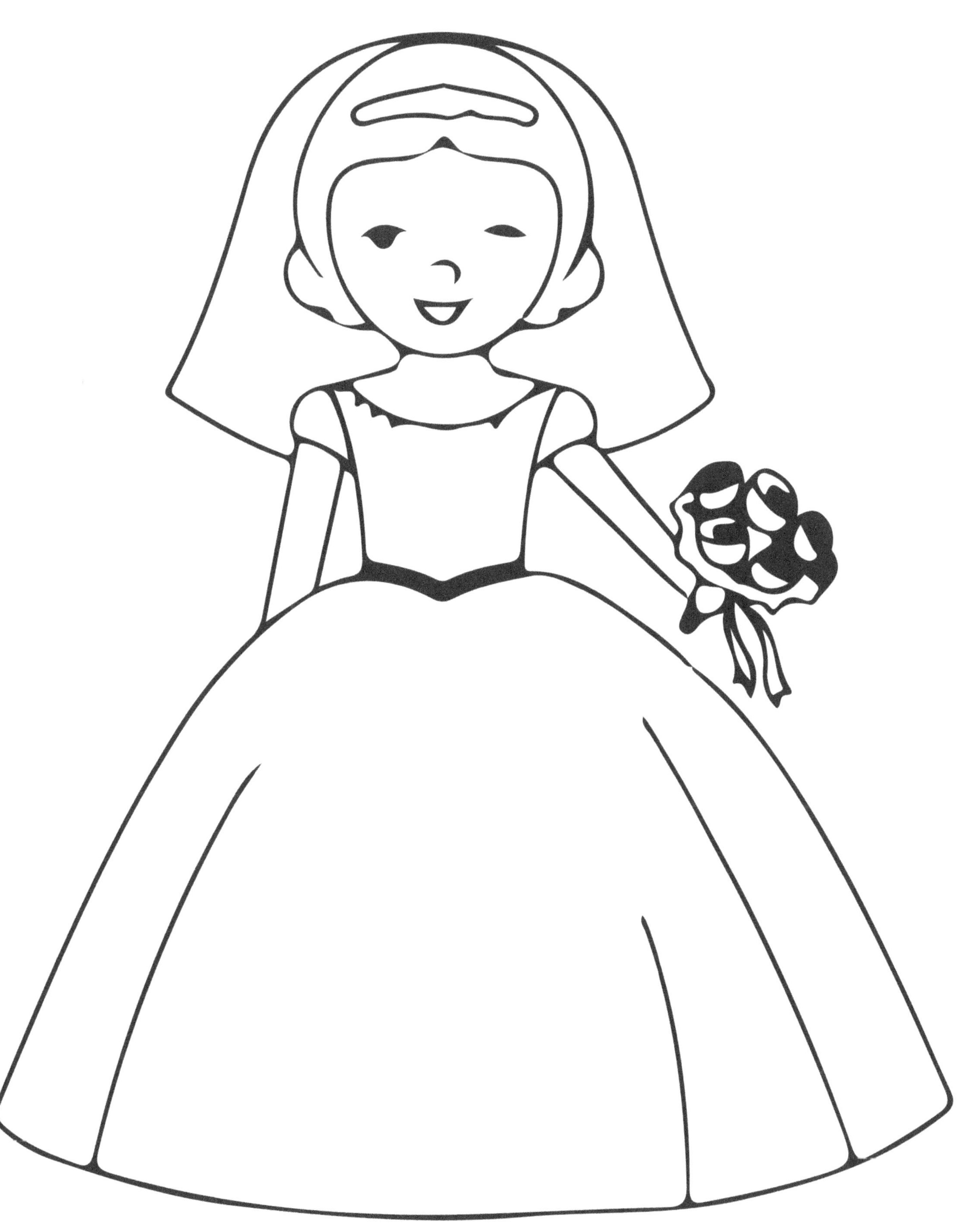

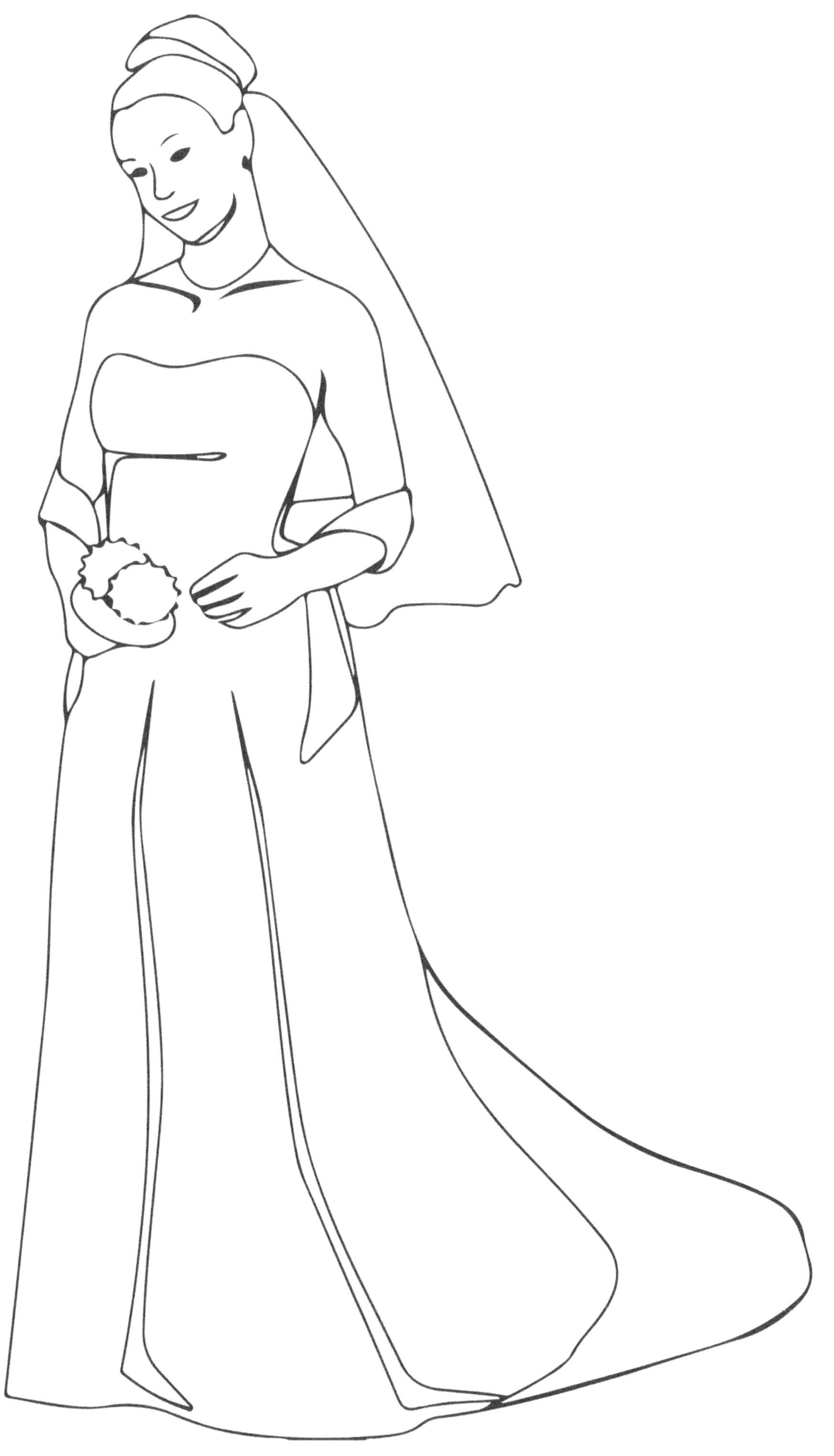

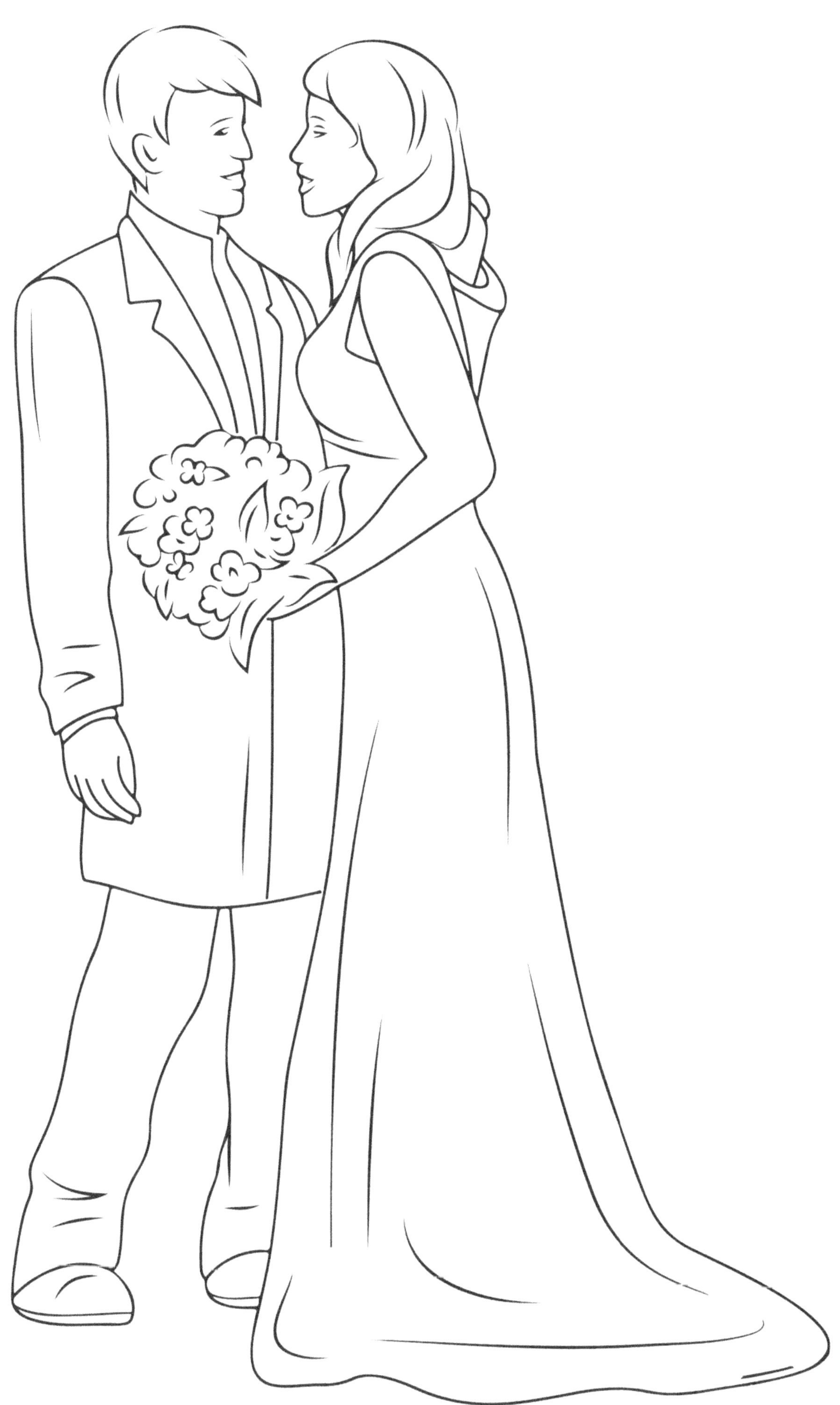

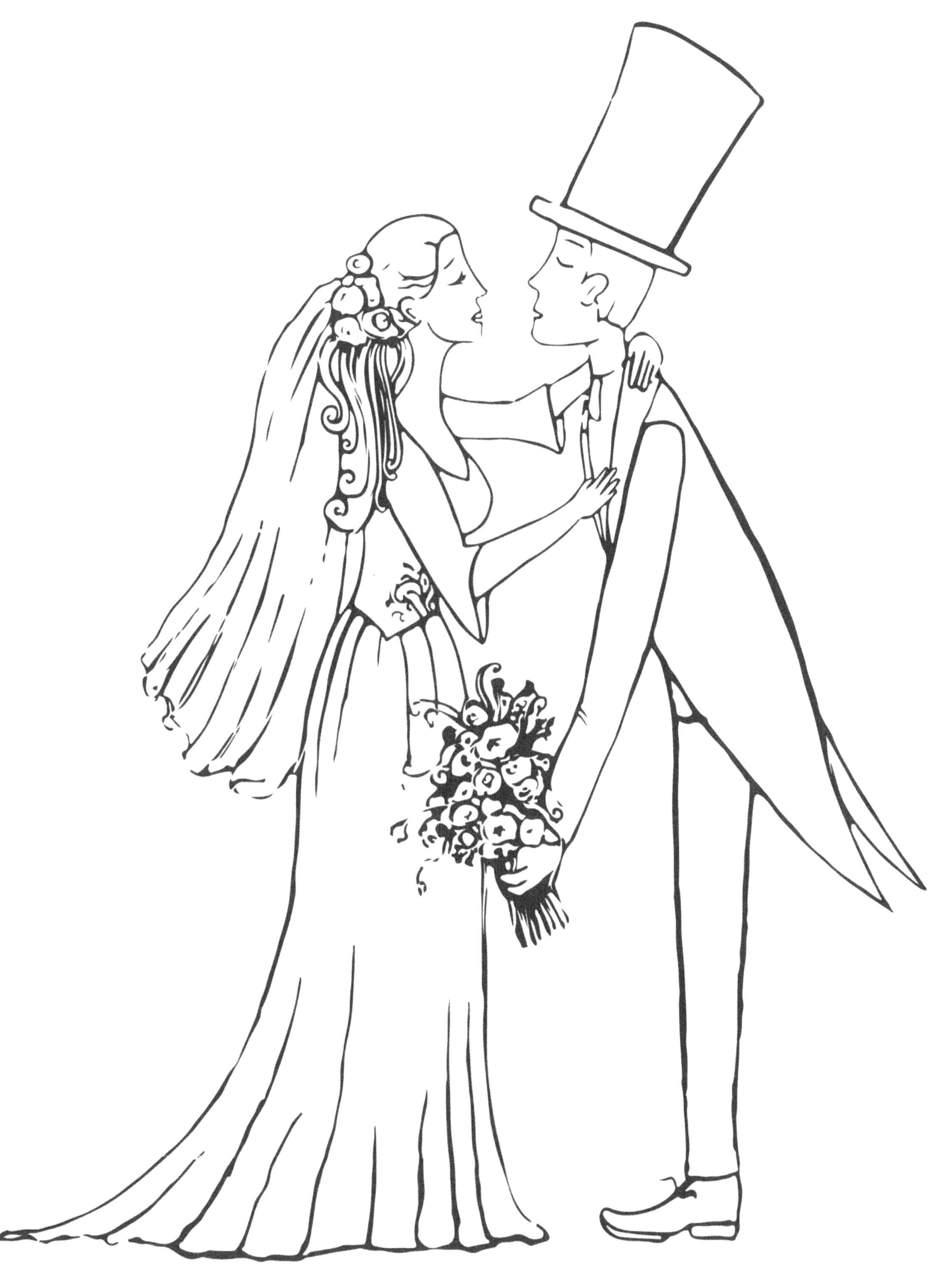

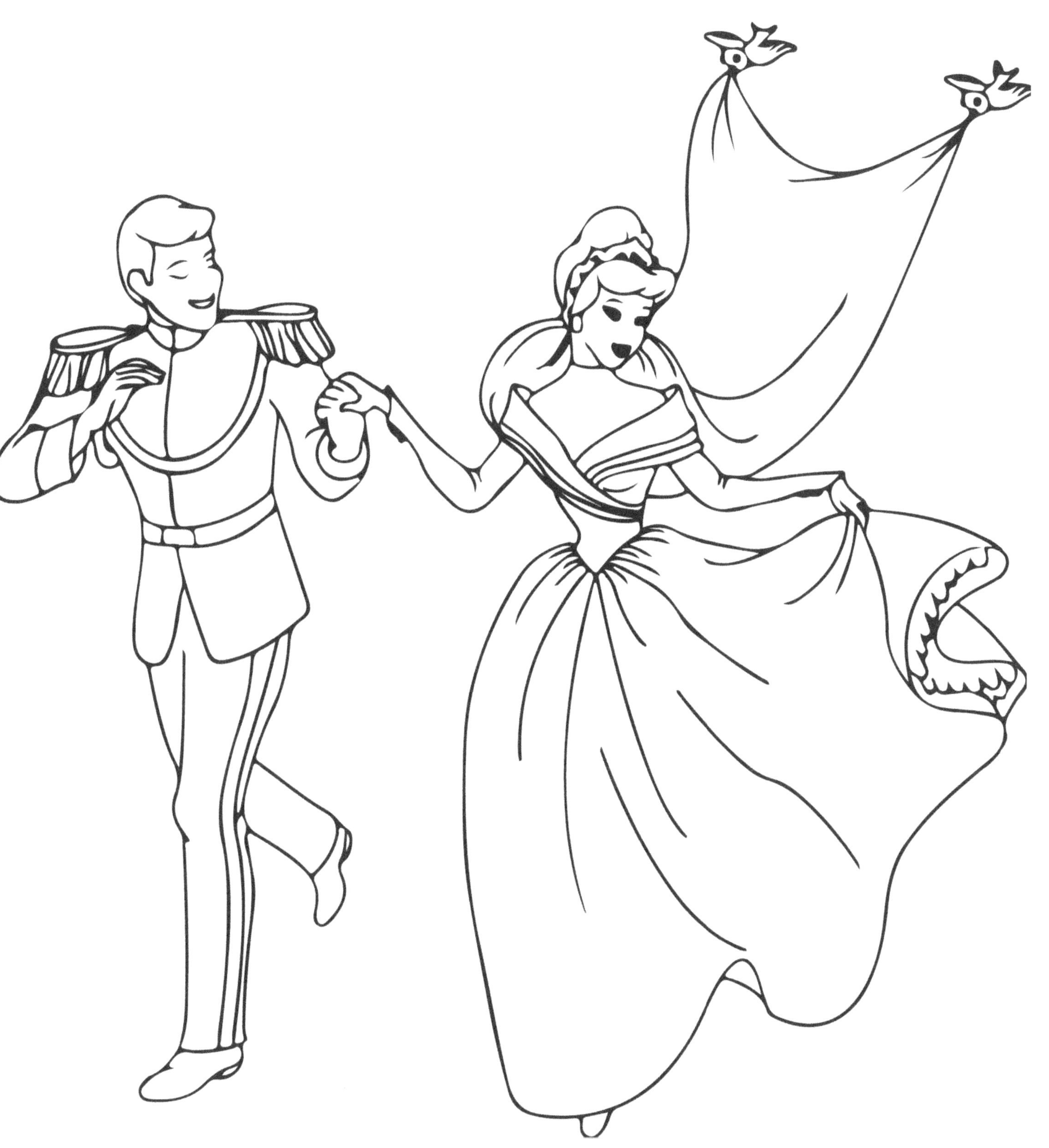

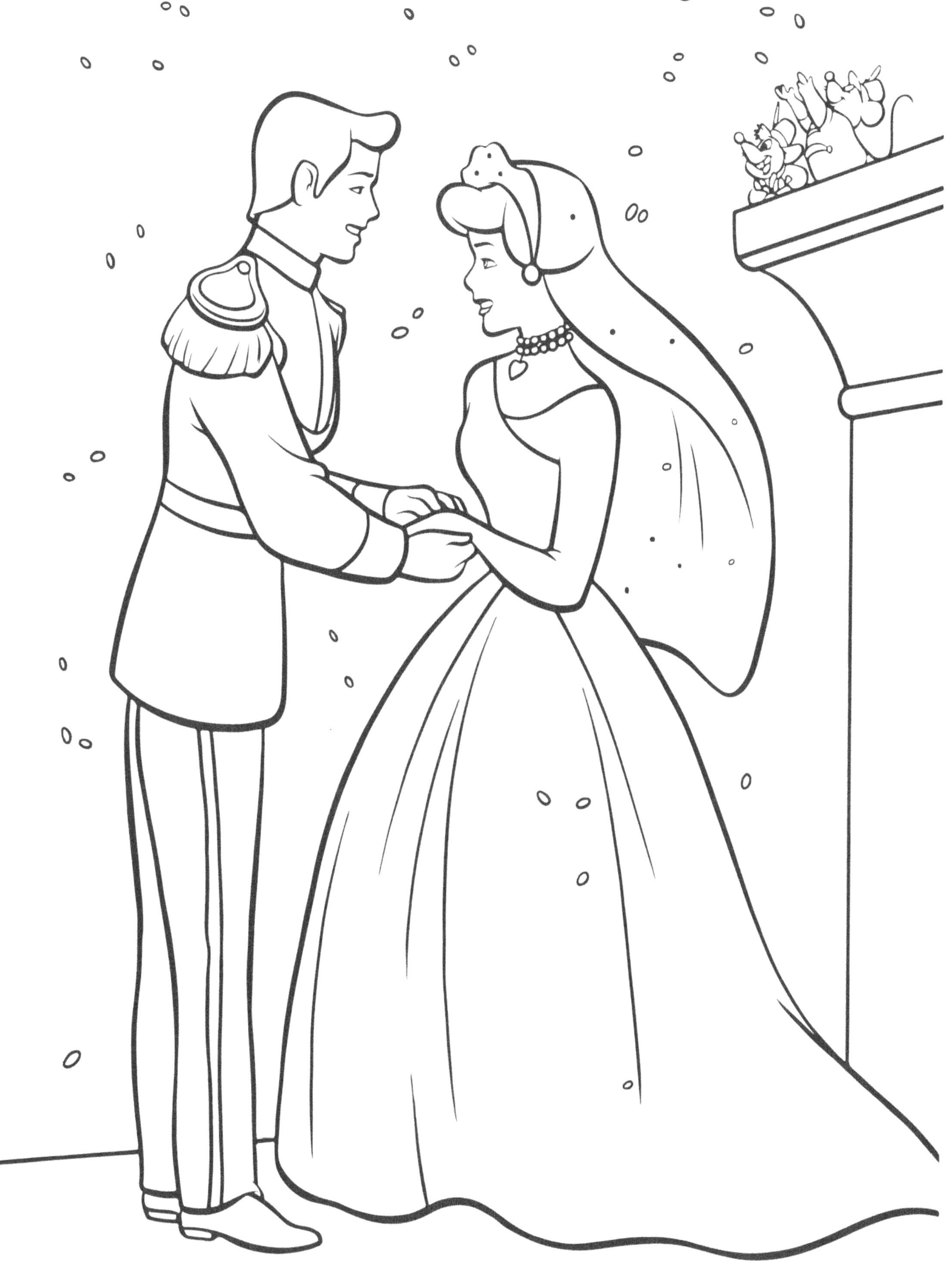

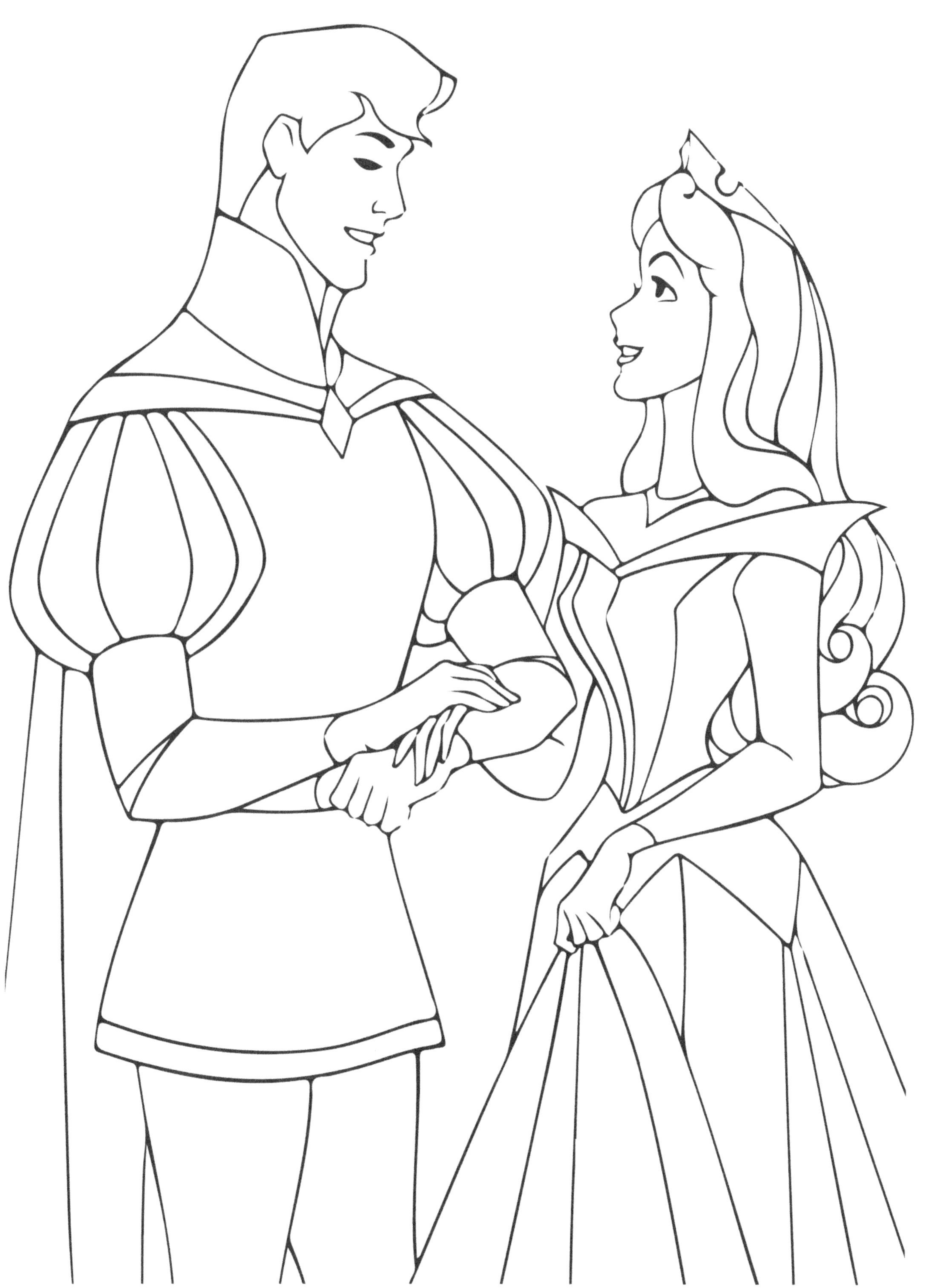

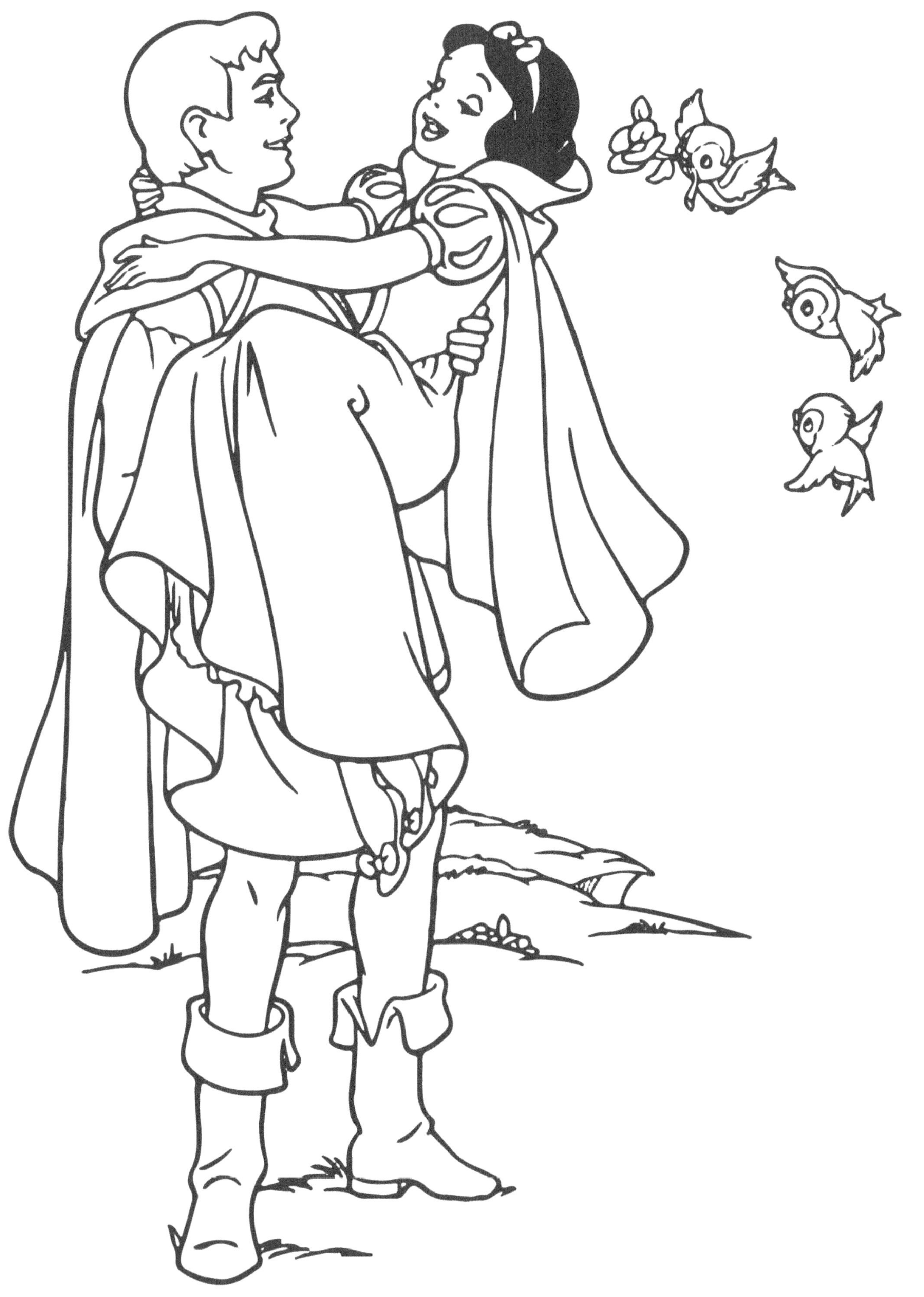

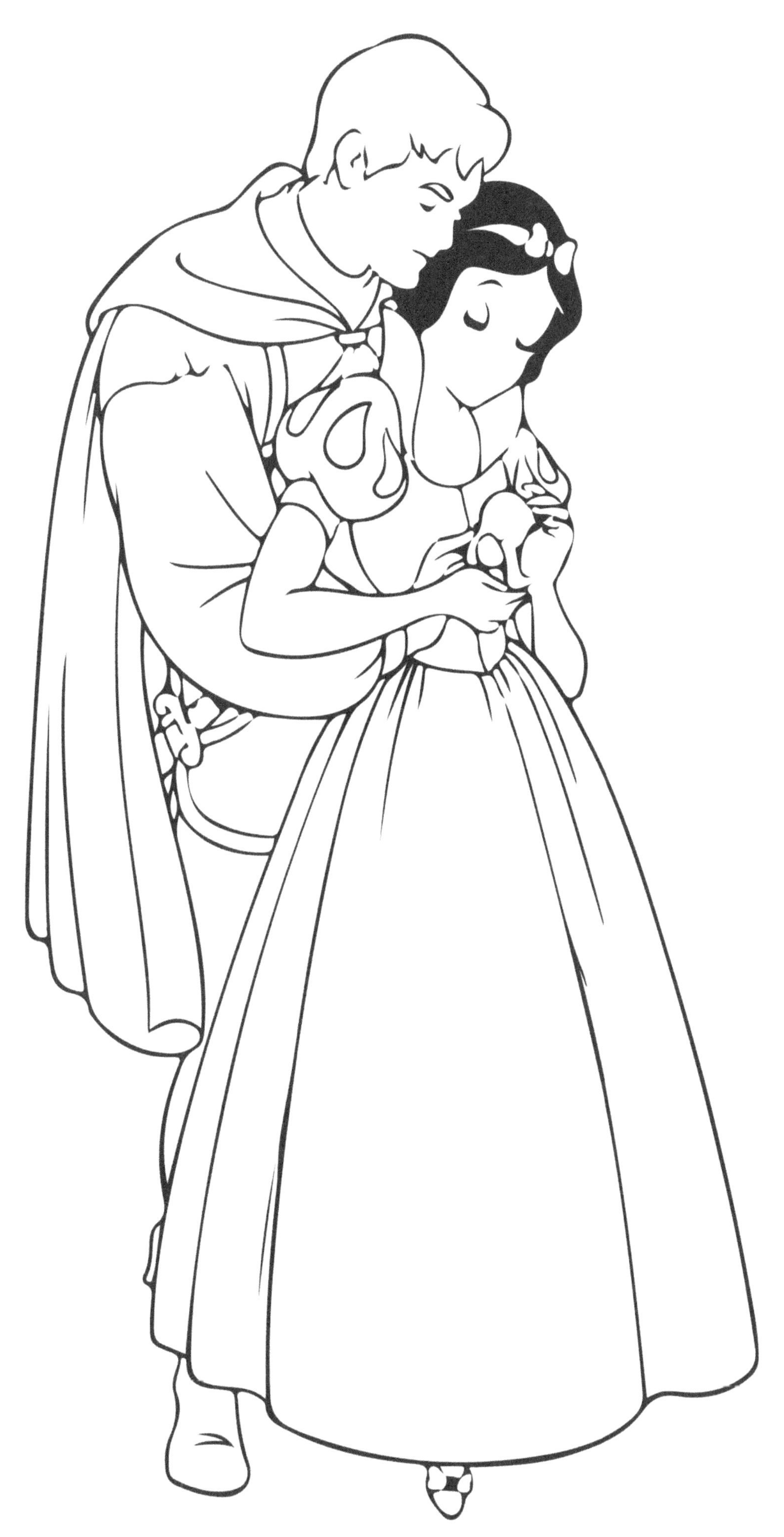

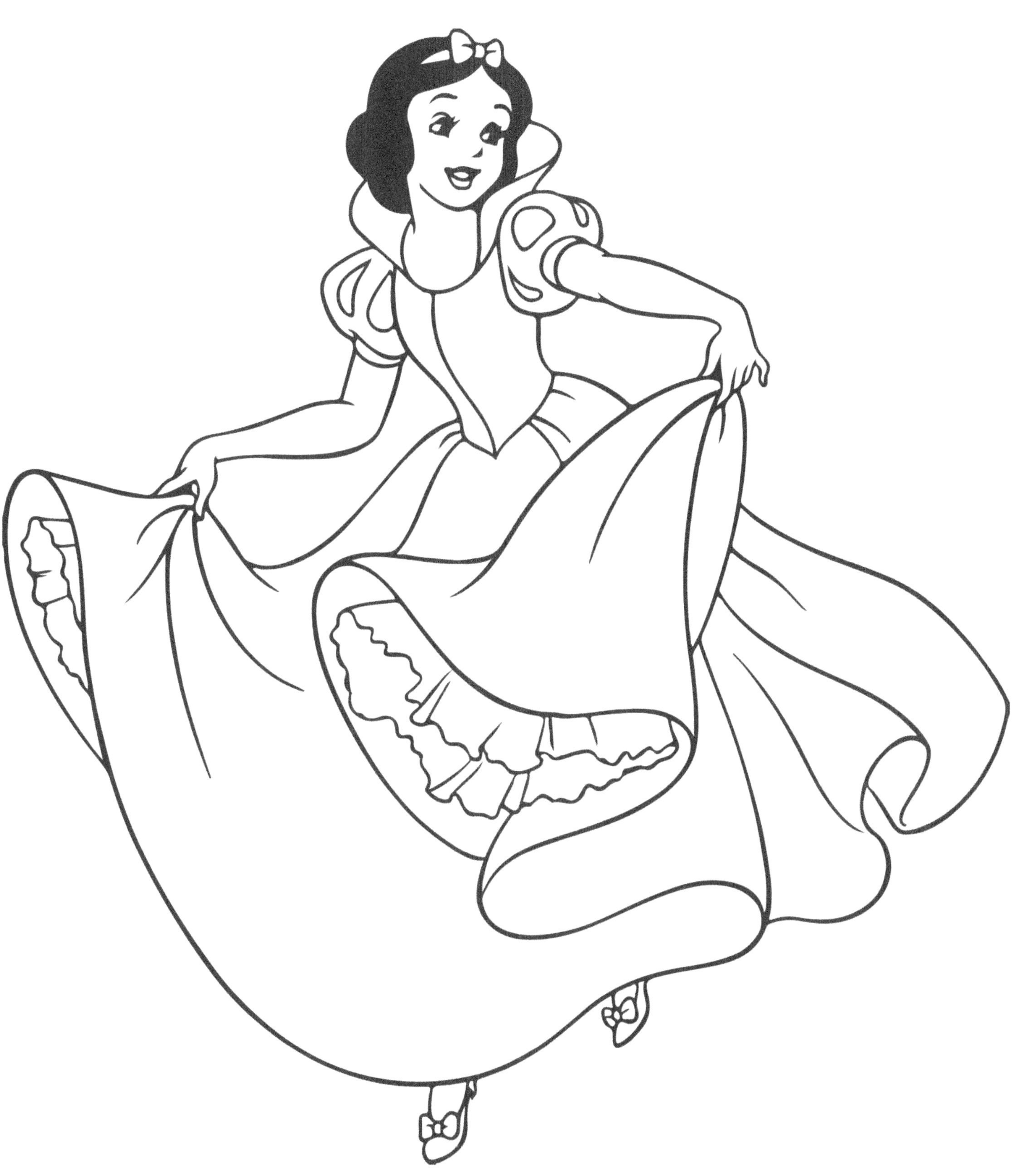

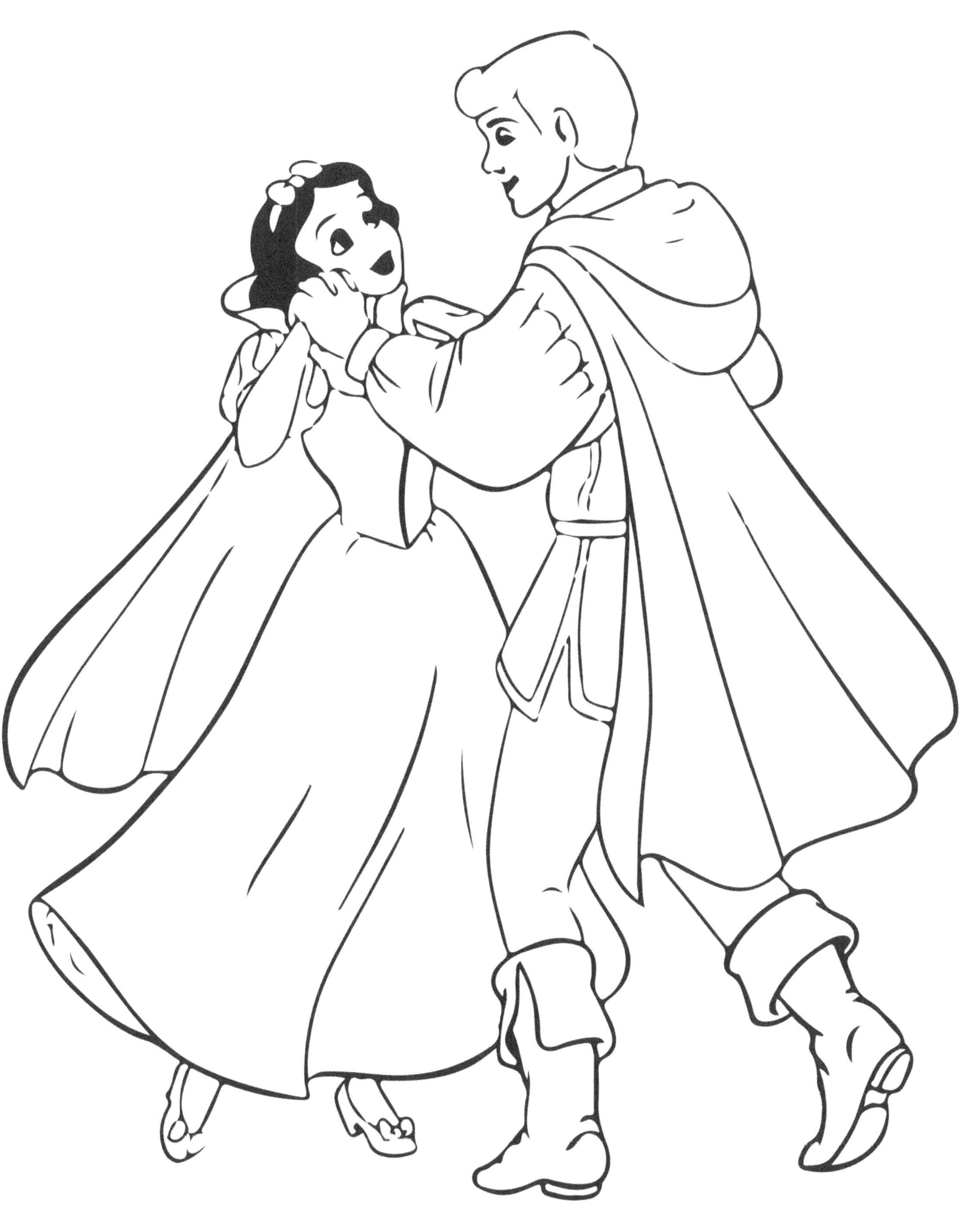